WISH AVE

WISH AVE

Alessandra Lynch

Alice James Books
New Gloucester, Maine
www.alicejamesbooks.org

10 9 8 7 6 5 4 3 2 1

Alice James Books are published by Alice James Poetry Cooperative, Inc.

Alice James Books
Auburn Hall
60 Pineland Drive, Suite 206
New Gloucester, ME 04260
www.alicejamesbooks.org

Library of Congress Cataloging-in-Publication Data

Names: Lynch, Alessandra, 1965- author.
Title: Wish Ave / Alessandra Lynch.
Description: New Gloucester, Maine : Alice James Books, 2024.
Identifiers: LCCN 2024020790 (print) | LCCN 2024020791 (ebook) | ISBN
  9781949944662 (trade paperback) | ISBN 9781949944389 (epub)
Subjects: LCGFT: Poetry.
Classification: LCC PS3612.Y54 W57 2024 (print) | LCC PS3612.Y54 (ebook)
  | DDC 813/.6--dc23/eng/20240513
LC record available at https://lccn.loc.gov/2024020790
LC ebook record available at https://lccn.loc.gov/2024020791

Alice James Books gratefully acknowledges support from individual donors, private foundations, the National
Endowment for the Arts, and the Poetry Foundation (https://www.poetryfoundation.org).

Cover art: "Waiting for Spring in Tompkins Park" by Metka Krašovec, 2000.

CONTENTS

[ONTO THE LIT DOORSTEP OF THE WORLD]

Onto the lit doorstep of the world, the first wave of shadows
fell—

Michiko had left the neighborhood. Green boxwood shining
in its corner. Lilacs— heavy pink in ruptured sacks.

In her wake, trees bloomed wordless. Seeds spun, cracked…
the wind hurried its sorceries.

Since I've been a child it's been difficult to breathe I said to you,
waves of shadows rising, falling….

You said our parting might be unforeseen.
You held my hand, pressed your face against mine.

Michiko gone, other neighbors breathless—.
Never not children, never not small, we float as petals and leaves,

dispersing as we drop. Look from any high ridge of universe
to find her—Michiko briskly walking her two small dogs in figure eights,

eyes serious, face abundant. I said *She was fed
by the sun.* Already the air began to turn and run—.

THE SPEAKER RUNS THROUGH SHADOWS

Charcoal-grey the shadows, sometimes the blue of gathered dust
I ran through a blur of them, soundlessly they'd fallen
around the others: branch-shadows, telephone-wire-shadows, sleety-shadows,
church-shadow, and the shadows of incorrigible fences where nothing was to
be kept in or out—.

       Indistinguishable some shadows one from the next, others well-
formed and painful to watch: torn-up shadow-mouths of fish, the battered
head of a shadow-dog,
the softness of crises past they were not ominous. I ran through
them so heavily I made a world of shadow. (If I could will myself
to fall as beautifully—.)

       There's the tiny shadow of that flower, foxglove, shadow-shelf for
rain, shadowy grass spikes on pale pave. Shadows flattened on the roads
we speed down, deposed from our meadow and its
numerous inscrutable shadows, separate in our sexless shadow-cars,
yielding, stopping, going as instructed by commodified light.

       What of the laughter of shadows? What of the respiratory shadows
of leaves blown by wind? The counterpoint of your shadow with the child's?—
merging, breaking apart, merging again.

                What of loneliness—

Great Signifier, shadow

                  of breath—?

[ARE WE THE DAUGHTER'S HANDS?]

Two Voices

Are we the daughter's hands?
…Folded as two dead birds? Then how

can we be speaking? Their wings speckled, so
…how dead could they be?!?

Exactly.
…Or are we the voices

in the yellowish field of the mind? Not likely.
…True. We're floating over a wedding bench in the Memorial Garden

facing the Tulip Tree,
…a wall of shrubbery behind us.

A gravel path mindlessly wanders through ground ivy, circles the tree
…should anyone need to situate us.

Is this where we began?
…Incipient Warriors of Time…

no beginning, only Ever
…as ever we are—.

Here is where we'll be even when rawed
…by winter or wrung out in sweat, stubborn

come summer's dread heat.
…If we're her hands, we're hanging like puppets.

Shhhh…speak for yourself!
….We're the hands that refuse to go numb.

We're the hands that remember
…and beyond that—I mean before that—

lyrical and inconclusive….

Two Voices Dispute Harmony Harmoniously

"To harmonize the whole—the task in art."
---You've been thinking of Kandinsky? Surges of yellow, blemished
    reds?

Blue horses, gashed hooves—
---but the music—almost Shostakovich—music in those shapes.

Where are we?
---Our Speaker's "living" room....

Look at that painting, torn-up greens, charcoals weepy above their
mantel.
---The fireplace—over the decades—was mouthy with flame just twice.

Just twice mouthy with flame while Kandinsky's colors roaringly
whipped above, wildness
---packed in a frame, a heavy golden glotted frame.

Who placed it there?
---Who nailed it?

They couldn't nail "to harmonize the whole"... there were four separate
rooms
---for the four separate people of the house the most dissonant being...?

She, the wife, the bearer of harmonies and High News, our Speaker!

---Four in the house. One moves and the others need to sway....

At least sway / at least roll up to her / at least query / or contend / or
fight / at least touch
---for a minute before dashing off

into the separate quarters
of the Heart.

We're moving fluidly from room to room much like Nightingale's
concerned lanterns....
---Here is the child with the stitched-up mouth, dark hole for an eye.

Here is the child, his barricare of books, green windows.
---Here is the adult-child tight-wound in a cold sheet.

Here is the child, the last child, our Speaker, curled
around four blankets, one sheet

sheared into three—
---the very "picture of neglect"—why aren't they

holding each other why aren't they in sync why aren't they eating meals
---or heading to the park or the church or the field why aren't they

looking into each other's eyes? Why are there four children, not two—?
---Why has nobody taken care?

Kandinsky was talking about art—not
---harmony among them.

That's their own lonely business, their own
---ferocity

to handle—

After a Massacre of Wrens, the Speaker Tells the Story of Michiko

Massacre of wrens on the sunporch—
        Blue eyelids of the buried
        Blue eyelid of our planet
Tint of bluish yolk

Several cities over, LOVE cropped up on cardboard signs. BE KIND.

        Michiko left the neighborhood—she'd given me a paper bag,
spotted caterpillars, a glass jar filled with leaves they could eat.
The clouds whitened merciless.
We sat in the pooling blood of our shadows.

Some days I will the planet to swallow us
and closer to its core we could become iron or shale. Often I will
us to be stiller, more harmless. We could re-form as fish,
velvet-eyed, blue-finned, quivering—.

        The caterpillars crawled out or died. Michiko would loop
round in beautiful extravagant loops,
feeding ferns and lilies to the neighborhood,
trilling "Hello Hello, beautiful day!"

We need to know her words to keep
humanity humane, break from
our dazed, stuttery circling....

The circles circling inside me now
sometimes sidle,
sometimes pop or thinly hiss—.
Sometimes I open my mouth and out they float,
gathering till they're dense blue as smoke.

In the dream someone offered to buy me a coat
but who was he. Without telling us, almost
on tiptoe, Michiko left the neighborhood—
unfettered bright safe word she was. She looped,
didn't circle....
    The remnant wren-fledglings clung to the screen,
    their nervous heads, darting eyes, one with a thrashed-up
    wing, the other, stump-legged.

Did you leave them a plate of water?
Would you bury them as you had the first?

    Michiko crouched
in the grass, hands in the dirt, spade by her side.
    Trickles
of wren-blood here and there on the porch. A spotty
massacre of poked-up feathers, bloody
beaks, toothpick bones, those opaque shields that were eyes,
pitted heads, all of it, the whole desecration
could fit in my hand.
    We overlooked
all of it "in the interest of...."

You must invent
a new language, a new universe to contain horror.

Michiko planted flowers
on every street in the neighborhood.

She pushed a small yellow wheelbarrow of bushes and saplings
down the street. So simply made you'd think
she'd suffer no collisions. "Hello Hello, beautiful day!"
Streaks of light in her hair,
on her cheeks.

"My daughter is a figure skater, my husband…." Here
she stopped speaking. Another fledgling now in the corner of the porch,
tiny beak open, half-wing aflutter, also maimed? She had to gather
herself before she could speak.

What does
their huddling mean, why did the well one stick by the sick one?
What do their flat wings weigh—?

"He no longer sings." She looked away. "He was a cellist
in the orchestra."

WE NEED TO PUT OUR HANDS INTO THE EARTH TO FEEL AGAIN

(A Voice, the Speaker)

Did you look at the Sturgeon Moon last night?

> *No, but it looked at me as I slept and for a moment floated a cool hand over my face*
>
> *while I dreamt of the ancient door*
> *and the modest iron key but mostly the wind, the wind*
>
> *lightly pacing, sometimes hurrying—*
> *carrying an Enormous Ear.*

[HOW TO PIECE IT TOGETHER]

(Two Voices)

How to piece it together—?
---The neighbor's butterfly bush grown enormous
            tagged with Hairstreaks, Swallowtails, even *Zegris*—
            sooty-orange-
            tipped butterflies from Turkey, her grown daughter
            enthralled.

---Can't see the blooms
            for the butterflies!

How by her mother's hands thrived seedlings, bare-root bulbs
stemming, twining, leafing—banishing the Lawn.

---Deadly as ever it has been: the Lawn.

And now the mother has—
---passed? Sorry sorry....

"I'm sorry too"
her daughter said sharply beneath her mask.
She also said "we're burying her ashes tomorrow"

---or did she say "scattering?"

Not sure but when the body's gone, it's
akin to a glasswing butterfly—

---brush-footed butterflies we are when the body's gone—
          as Michiko's as Jean's as Milton's

When the body's gone—
as Philomena's as Linda's....

PAUSE

---the names remain, the voices sure as safety pins,
clairvoyant, each sweetly
clairvoyant, their Voices still speaking
to us, saying again and again "beautiful" "thank you" "I can't
imagine...."

---We were privy to their lower registers,
                    the shifting textures of their voices, how intimate....

We were inside their throats as they spoke!
They were inside our ears! How intimate this speaking!

---Who is to say their lives aren't more alive now
               or more clearly recognizable?

Don't say that to the daughter—
she's "burying her ashes tomorrow."

---She has her mother's ashes now—.
               Not all of us have this privilege.

What we have of our bereaved is their name, their voice
---no longer blocked or distracted by the body—pure!—distilled

essence of self!

---You are trying to convince yourself
                    out of grief?

I am trying to console
the two of us.

---Voices without bodies as we are,
Guardians of the House

---of the living of the dead.
We fill the pitchers with roses, pale orange, red.

---The dead roses stand alert,
the glass vases turn yellow…we are watchful for

---any transformation for any transformation suggests
movement and movement is

---living—remember Milton leaving
               messages in the yellow mailbox?

In summer, to open the door, he'd have to push
the overgrown wildflowers to the side

---always gently, always delivered letters
(CHORUS) with care…

I'd never heard a deeper voice in a mailman, basso surely!
---Nor I—imagine—a mailman

(CHORUS) with the name of a poet—!!

14

BRIDGE

What is at stake for us?

i.

---What is at stake for us?
I don't know, should we travel back?
---In time, do you mean, or away from this garden?
This garden's the only plot we've got.
---I am losing sensation in my feet. (Do we have feet?)
Too much material between your skin and the dirt.
---Oh, we are recounting the ancient story?
It is a young story—not so long ago we were stones. . . .
---Speak for yourself, I was a root—.
Well then, we'd better start there.
---There?
At the quick. I don't mean to startle you—.
---Who is that sound?
What is the wound?
---Always hunched in the dark poking at the wound.
A lake in Roethke's poem.
---Roethke was a lake—oh how he shuddered, swelled up—
how he roared to meet the storm!
---Can we take one glinting hurt at a time before we're swarmed—?

ii.

They're really close.

How far are they?

Close enough. You smell their breath?

Yes, not winterberry. Vodka and juniper-smoke.

I don't want to be here.

Back away. They'll stick
like shadows. You have to do
something clever.

Like?

Go underground. Bear it up
with the eyeless nosing things.
You're no flower, but you can
breathe with the roots.

I won't forsake my eyes.

Then return to the old dream—
polar bears swimming in a winter sea,
stained fur moving through blue icebergs…
two young ones. Return to that,
eyes closed.

Will Michiko ever come back?

Why would she? You didn't speak her language. The neighbors
across the street ignored her.

She loved the sky with me, the sunlight, birds, I gave her a boxhedge bush.
We both pressed our hands in the dirt.

Is that enough to live by?

It's how she lived—without
her husband's music, the acute cut of her daughter's
skate.

iii.

What happened when you had the baby
---Cake became a beautiful word almost spiritual. I began closing my eyes
when I ate it

You ate it
---Well, I ate the icing and the thinnest layer of cake below it

You didn't finish any of the pieces
---I didn't finish any of the pieces

Did you want to
---Another empty plate, scraped? No

After the baby was born
---My legs slackened lost impetus. Once I ran, ran, oh how I went running
the glistening miles forest trails I became animal I became topography
purpose was beyond the point

How do you feel now when you're full
--- *Failured like a misbegotten rose espaliered but with dull human eyes*
that shine on the baby when he begins to eat and sing and rock

iv.

Yeah, I'm scared of everything—true—
But I am looking at the painting
Where blue and white
Make silver. Oh that
Little crooked mouth
Oh, it's nearly speaking
Or sighing but I am here, here
I say to it, I am here,
Rest your head on the other
Sectors of paint,
I will make sure your thin
Bluish-white neck
Is safe. Dearheart,
Being so open this way and here
In the dirtiest month
Of winter, I love you,
Vulnerable one. Hold
Your face as though it is
A flower,
Grievous-seeming,
A hole in your cheek,
Your ears blotted out,
The narrow exhausted
Anguish of your eyes

And the mouth so small
I'll need to feed you bit by bit
Small portions of the world
So you can live
In it.

v.

The child spun out of the baby
Made many pencil drawings when he was nine
Of faces with bandaged eyes
Two bandages on each eye, two crosses over each
What had they seen that cut them?
Were they bandaged to stop seeing?
I thought there was a red droplet
On one of their faces
It could have been a mistake
It could have been a mistake the child kept there
Boneflowers grow low outside his window
Blood rushes into the maples
I will try not to talk about it

vi.

Don't talk about it he said
---he didn't talk?

There was too much talky un-talk around him
---or what would he say or feel
when he was saying the what, the who

before she left
For weeks and weeks he wore the t-shirt Michiko
gave him
till the chocolate spills and ketchup
and crumbs from the cake made a camouflage

---(protect us from the world, o wordlessness)

vii.

It's like paint outside
And the sink's overflowing
Not out of abundance
But from a trepidatious leak.
The paint is blue-white, the paint
Is cold. Face it: the paint is snow.
The failure in melting
The gone-done of it
The globular shame in it,
You're at war
With the cycle. Been at war
With your body for centuries
And still—you're at war with the sea
When you're at war with your body
And you're at war with your
Aging and you're at war with
The trees…howsoever you are
And whoever you are—dictators
Or dictatorees. Or me. I'm at war
With my body, I'm at war with
The sea which won't have me

Which won't let me breathe
I'm at war with the cycle, at
War with the wind, at war with my
Wound at war from within—
It's like pain outside
And the sink's a wreck
And I'm sinking in it
Not out of heaviness
But a fearful leak
And the paint is escaping
And the snow is on the melt
And where will the bears go
There was a poet once
Generous and kind and tall and red-haired
And terrified
Who opened her freezer door
And said to them
"Climb"—

viii.

What if you walk with a lantern tonight
    through the dark air, loose dead hairs swirling around you
Do you mean snow?
---Yes and those who accompany snowfall
Jean?
---Jean and Michael as children walking through their separate forests
Singing as they walked?
---Singing, yes, singing
But very softly the way children do for the trees to hear them
---Very softly, yes, hushed their voices in the thin wild air

Those soft-singers what were they trying to make disappear?
---And so young already
  to be wanting to be part of the Great Vanishment
I hurt Michiko

PAUSE

---With purpose?—
No, but with great carelessness
---Surely wherever she is...
But I carry it, I carry it like a wounded tree, a shaven birch
---Write in chalk or pencil, write the hurt out
Chalk, pencil, the weaker cousins of ink
---What if you walk outside with a lantern tonight
  Then will she reappear?

PAUSE

And then may I take her hands
they're small you know, a bird could slip through them
---Small hands know about care, about being careful
Small, she is purpose, always striding round the neighborhood even when she's
not there
---Is that why you're drifting
You can see that?
---Yes, you're all loose dead hairs swirling
If she's forgotten the hurt I caused, is it gone
---We hurt only ourselves
What about bad presidents? What about those in the slaughterhouse?
And our mothers?
---Let's go now, let's take a gander at the horses in high wind on that hill
  from five years ago

24

We'll take the lantern and walk through loose dead hairs
of snow, we'll accompany
snowfall and Jean, Michael, and Michiko...
---Set at ease in the forest

(Set at ease in all the music of the trees—)

BRIDGE

The Speaker Shares a Story with One Voice

Drenched green were the trees at night,
the music building a warm pear-gold blur....
We walked through the rain to get there—.

---Were you in pain?
I was in Stark, no soft occlusion
---despite the rain?

Despite the rain and its flickering ingenuities, no
---respite in rain?

No respite there. The boy had seen my dark eyes, my floating—.
---Was it your spirit, was it your heart that floated?

I'm not sure what part but he saw something troubled, I might float off
---Is that what you wanted?

Too much in Stark to know about want, want had
        all but consumed me....

---Were you the milk or snow
of want?

---Something more deadly—something in the nightshade family....
Whatever I say feels like a lie except for the straight story—.
---Go on, go on....

The boy asked if I wanted to go to the piano room
while he practiced. We walked through the drenched green—
      dark thrushes asleep in the trees—
to the warm gold blur of a building
itself a musical note, an inscape….
We entered the dark room that stayed
dark, he went straight to the piano
while I stood for a moment

---feeling wrong?
I stood for a moment in my floating my floating like a quivering cloak….

---All the people you thought you were protecting…
I was not among them, the boy was
playing the piano, the air drenched green,
the dry thrush and the wind now picking up

---All the sounds of our small world
tearing through his fingertips on those velvet keys, velvet-on-bone….

---And you?
I am on the memory-floor soft and sad a small billow of listening
---to the piano, to the rain…

to my loneliness. I'd come into that room
---for love.

Anytime I followed anyone it was
---for love.

Listening so hard to his playing so hard we were for a time entirely absorbed
---it was the music he was loving…

yes, I was a floating bundle of listening and I heard
every note of his love

for the music. That he brought me with him
through drenched green to the soft gold house of music

---was a knowing of real human love

My mother could have been a concert pianist
---instead she became?
A lawyer. Her soul, her genius for sound became
---pure listening?
Rapturous listening to music. I was a very quiet child.
---She might not have heard you...
unless I shouted or said something about music....

---The boy was gifted?
Worlds rushed through his fingers, sensations, empires of feeling
---and in that brilliant music? In that brilliant sound?

I rose and left the room without his knowing.

[OUR GRIEVANCE IS…]

Two Voices

Our grievance…or one of them…is
…that we can't touch

a table or a husk
…another's hand—yours, for instance….

Mine? You've wanted…?
…for Centuries or More to put my hand on yours

For us to have hands!
…We who have a hand in things but none of that

flesh or bone. We couldn't even bleed
…when most hurt. Or love in anysoeveryway

when touch is essential
…essential to be gentle, to be harsh….

Explosions, implosions—
…a firmament of fire in the sea—

a Turner painting,
…lost limbs the thrashing….

We move like music you and I,
…we touch like music I and you.

We fight as music—
...I love you.

We don't tuck our anger away—.

...Let's not tuck away the heart of anything
     but release it as

incrementally?
...As judiciously as the sun might edge into the sea

as judiciously as if
....our lives depend on it.

CROWN HILL CEMETERY
(The Voices in Chorus & the Speaker)

---Were we with you in Crown Hill Cemetery?
Yes, a fair way away—two tombstones facing each other
marked: BARNETT and LOVE

and frozen near those stones: two deer in the grass:
a spotted Doe a Stag, perfectly

sylvan, unwavering.

---It was the first day you had ever eaten
in a cemetery.

A friend loses her father he loses his brother nothing in order,
losing our mothers all of us their senses our senses lost—.

---And there you were eating.

I don't know what I want with ghosts....

---The dead always closer than it seems...

and we distant as that rushing blue fountain that rises,
falls backs, ashamed of its ardor.

PAUSE

---Remember walking away

from the infant's grave on the steepest crest in Crown Hill
Cemetery…?

From the infant's grace. He'd never had
a voice.

PAUSE

---But there arose two enormous hands—

two enormous marble hands
their fingertips touching, seven starlings could rest on each finger,
and the shadow those giant hands made—

---two giant birds, two deer in the grass—

a spotted Doe! a Stag!

---Silence is its own voice.

We can hear the spirit-infant now in every room,
in astronomical star-wet fields.

---He's grown into a child with serious eyes,

wearing a navy blue coat that he buttons slowly, with care,
like a very old man.

Thousands of miles away
his quiet
carries---

---He's the death within us, breathing, rustling about,
    ancient and unborn.

The spotted Doe, the Stag,
    their quiet carriage, unbearable

---Music—

IRE

(The Speaker *Sotto Voce*)

It's got to be somewhere your anger and
like the moon though very far away still leaves
an impression, is apt to hover
  by the bedroom window a child stares through
from disheveled blankets. All throat. No voice.
  You know how violent that anger can get—
a whitened rat, wide as a slap, a chickadee brambled in the barb,
  the cheek gashed from the brass bull slung
at a wineglass. Somewhere you must
  have a moon-and-anger gang
too loud to hear, too close to feel.
  Those hoodlums stuffing a stealth of leather into a scream.
Some things shine only
when they're in opposition. That anger quiet
as the near-dead,
  near-dead as the moon, quiet
as a thistle seething beneath the lake,
  quiet tasting like a bullet,
the metallics of pure air. Nothing pure
  about your atmosphere.

  Quiet shelf, book-quiet. Readers talking about the death
of quiet. You know. Doctors talking in hushed tones
about what happens to anger when its quiet goes

Boozeflower

(The Speaker & One Voice)

I can't say "I can't do this anymore—" anymore....

    ---Sure you can.

It's no longer truthful...Richard's painting is hanging on the wall.

    ---Was it ever the truth?

It was a necessary cry...from my throat, not my gut. His paint is magical.
.

    ---All stones are beautiful, sometimes unnerving. Can you live inside a painting?

Fine. I <u>can</u> say I can't do this anymore...then what?

    ---Humans can be mercurial, frivolous, but when they get their hands in the right place....

Richard created water on an utterly flat surface—slow-moving water
with gleam and depth
where a dark crag rises, where the island and its huddled trees wait—
not like Mars....
    ---Are you drinking?

The sky is dark as wine outside my window, yes, and the candle
and its reflection—

flick, flick—move forward together. Rowing through the water in Richard's
painting is my striving, I will use oars the exact color of the light on his water.

     ---Don't let the hanging frame stop you from entering that
world.

Thirst is a need, isn't it?

     ---You have whatever a lifetime is to retreat or fly over the thing
         you could have loved. How fluid this fire, how fluidly
           whirl the dust and particles
             that make a planet.

     SILENCE

     ---Are you drinking?

It is personal…boozeflower, this roving over Mars, gin-berry, bowls of alcohol
that line a burning hallway… Nothing not curved or blurred….

     ---That kind of scorch lives in the ancestral ditch—have
mercy—.

Do you believe in the sanctity of family? Do you believe in blood?
Richard drinks only one glass at night with dinner.

     ---You know what I mean, booze cuts your mind to rat-
     feathers….

I want to hold each oar firmly—it takes tenderness to row through—.
When I drink I talk to the grandfather who floated through holidays in his
invisible gown—his vanishing worse than Michiko's. She gave me three

39

redbud trees, he gave me his lineage which in his sober mind he wouldn't hand out to anyone.

---And your own father?

*He retells his past righteously, so he omits details—paralyzing omissions—
his brother—not killed in a motorcycle accident as said—but died an addict,
OD'd, my once-met uncle OD'd possibly on heroin, he was the black sheep,
the scapegoat,
nobody really liked him, so he became a cop and OD'd....*

---The alcohol is not making you soft tonight.

*The alcohol is a porthole, it is round glass, storm and fog and furious
white gashes.
My ship's in tumult—Rimbaud a stowaway—clanking skidding ridden with
starfish, fractured
as Mars, as a rover roaming over Mars—.*

---Why didn't you do something other than drink tonight?

*I'm scared of my own capability—I've neglected my grandfather, Michiko,
my father, the cat, the planet. I haven't seen Richard in decades—but Richard
too.*

*And I'm sad about the optimism of the Old Masters. How did they see the
sky? Did they consider Mars a good place to send a rover? Snow barely falls
before melting, white welts mid-air—*

---Richard preserves a glint of the planet for us to remember.

SILENCE

    ---You can say you can't do this anymore but you'll keep doing
it. Anyone who says or thinks that will keep doing it.

It's a cop-out like my uncle cop who OD'd anonymously.
They propped his body on a motorcycle and turned the ignition and already
dead he roared away—.

    ---Wordless, Michiko breathed color into the flowers.

PAUSE

    ---Go wordless with me toward the deflated sun, the sunken
clouds. Stand near a tree, bow down.

I'll drop my glass for that—.

The Unmedaled Medaling

(One Voice Addresses the Speaker)

---Someone's shadow sinks in a chair upstairs.

Where are the children?

---One hallway over.

I don't know what to do. Where to go. Are they safe?
Is anyone? Does a sinking shadow make a noise?

---What do you hear?

Awaiting a cue from the children—or maybe from the shadow in its chair—.

---What is outside?

A trellis and a ladder.

---Go outside then. Hang clematis and dark-eyed juncos from one.
Climb the other—

to the dead branch above the low house?

---To a star. You need to pay attention now to one thing at a time.

The cat is crying.

---She's old. She's near her time.

"Her time"—death? I don't want time then.

---Time is a stone in a pocket. It's a cold poker. A runway, a gangplank.

I want the stone from your sentence but nothing else. I wish the dreadful shadow would reach the bottom already. This sinking is unnerving....

---Does a shadow reach bottom when done sinking?

I want it to vanish. I want the cat to sleep on the chair.

---You once ran.

Was that a kind of sinking?

---Did you reach bottom?

I ran and ran and ran till I raced and medaled I raced and medaled ran raced medaling and medaling and medaling. There wasn't a bottom to that—

---you didn't feel victorious?

Not then not now.

---If you didn't care about winning, what did you want?

To unmedal. Vanish. That old tune. Not reach the bottom, sink below bottom.

---It's something like your son says in the songs he makes:

"I want to die but I don't want someone to kill me...."

---Could be shame.

Could be a wishbone. I want to move toward a book. I can still hear the shadow sinking. I'm restless.

---You are sitting in stillness.

I want to be a stone

---under riverwater?

Or sea.

---How simple.

How elemental and beautiful.

---Why the ladder? Why a trellis—?

The only things keeping me

---alive?

They're structures that could dissolve a shadow, send its particles where they belong. They are directives without

---imperative.

Yes, together they are

---a lullaby---.

Shhhhh. I think the shadow's done with its sinking.

---It's hovering over us, listening---

SOME OTHER MUSINGS BY THE VOICES

It's best to stay hidden in a drawer of light

      ---or a painting with a daffodil's shadow stretching across

or wherever. She is sad as plywood today. Sadder than what's pressing
into it—.

      ---You mean the drill or the saw?

I mean the day pressed to day.

      ---Her tarot read rock bottom and ruin....

Also transformation.

      ---Does one supersede?

Does "one" have enough air to breathe?

      ---People are not breathing well, she is not....

When you say that, we are no one not a one—. Do we even breathe?

      ---Do we know ourselves as indistinguishable from the next

or how soft we are, how easily done-for....

---I want to be sure to play keys as chords—.

That might comfort her. Now a dire stillness in the room.

---Is that a shadow at my elbow?

It is our Speaker. She's risen out of the wood.

---Though she doesn't feel like moving.

Sleep then, dear piano.

WOEBEGONE A FUNNY WORD AT FIRST TILL THE ARTILLERY AND EYELESS HORSES AND THE CHILD DRAWING SMILING DEVILS *HAHAHAHAHAHA*
(One Voice, the Agitated Speaker)

---Was he making peace with his demons?

Demons foisted upon him, demons crawling out of bomb shelters, long reptilian tails, curling, incurling, uninjured....

---What is the injury and where?

A full-body thing, I think, a thing of hunger in the grey village.

---How many civilians, how many civil people were there around him?

Grandfathers tending the shell-shocked, children mothering children....

SILENCE

I have just this window-smudge to peer through—I can only see them in parts....

---Are they alive?

As any part of anything lives. The worm. Forsythia branch in a cup of water.

---It is spring. There are demons and wars.

It is spring. I live with an injured child. He makes nests on the floor by the heating vent. He's building a shelter in his closet.

---How hard hit and by whom?

A combination of highly visible and deeply unseen forces—a parental regiment.

---So, you hurt him. How?

Not teaching him the spell of knives, not keeping a clean space

---for?

For thought, for self, for salve.

---Here is a place for weeping, here is a need to sweep....

Shell-shocked: magnolias splitting, soft carcasses—

---concussive the sweet briar, robins the color of old blood.

Explosive the child, wrapped in bandages, one bad eye untended.

---How can you bear yourself.

SILENCE

Not ready for that question. I'm ghostswept soldier, half-wind, half-ice—.

---Were you part of the bombardment?

I tore out daffodil bulbs before they stemmed thinking they were extricable, that I was unearthing space for the "real bulbs."

---A woman buried her husband in a flowerbed. He had diabetes.

Should I feel this as a sweet gesture?

---It was not her choice to bury him there, to bury him not her choice.

You're trying to bring me back to the literal? Will metaphor-making kill the planet?

---Metaphors do what they do—softly—with exquisite precision removing tumors in soft plosives while the patient or soldier looks through a smudge of window—.

The injured child lost track of his window. He had no way to look out

---for himself?

Hyacinth and honeysuckle fuming below his sill, a magnolia wand occasionally waving, blowing its petals across the glass....

---How can you bear it.

Are you listening to me?

---Yes

[Was that a dream we had?]

(Two Voices)

Was that a dream we had?
...Now we're floating over a field in
    a Fish and Wildlife area,
    floating over marshfields where Sandhill Cranes

poke around for crayfish and snails, then rest their slender necks—
...indefatigable reflections glimmering....

When you say "indefatigable," I think of Plath. Are they in crisis?
...As we—

????????
...The Human Voice, the art
        of conversation? In crisis, yes. And the Sandhill Cranes
        rising en masse over ice-tufts, gleaming. How wide an eye
        does it take to perceive birdfeet, a human body, the burning
        forest, polar bears all as one? Trillium, Allium,
        the Sea, flagellum....
        Snow as the ghosts of stars, Stars, the ghosts of knowing....

What are we doing here?

....We're here to track the Spirit of the Speaker...impossible without
        more world flooding in
        as she wrests herself awake....

It might take "all the music of the spheres"
to awaken humans
to themselves, to the earth—.

…A poignancy in her efforts
to rouse herself—

Trying to Find Michiko: The Speaker Speaks to Someone She Thinks is Michiko

---*The rosebush can go there—on the southeast side, Michiko*

Last night I heard the wind, or were those human screams?

---*I'll put the rosewood heartbox beneath the window*

Screams like my tiny dog screamed, hanging from the hawk's beak, small as a leaf, a screaming leaf

---*Should I use a trellis for the roses?*

SILENCE

---*I'm losing your voice, Michiko*

I'm not Michiko. I'm several masks beyond her

---*The screams weren't the hawk's weren't your tiny dog's weren't a leaf's and not yours*

Oh?

---*Once an icicle suspended from the northwest eave could scream*

Once a child…

---How can I begin to mourn....

You want Michiko to return. You want to talk about roses. How to plant them. Where...

---I want to thank her for the two redbud trees she planted, one for each child in this story.

What other recourse than to fill the neighborhood with screams? Nobody else would

---speak?

They stopped washing their bodies, they ate too much or nothing.

---I want Michiko back. I want to show her the bright-eyed rabbits hidden in boxwood, red-hearted cardinals the children's favorites....

The rosebush can go on the southeast side. There will be sun—
And from young honeysuckle branches, a trellis—

BRIDGE

[HELLO]

(Two Voices)

Hello
---Hello

Something hollow, something...
---scraped?

about our voices
        when they're alone

---Something scripture about
        our voices when
        alone....

Each one
        floating up trailing a colorless squiggly tail

---or a yellow-green
        ribbon, the voice is
        a ribbon flickering
        whether there's wind
        or not. Were you...

are you...

In chorus: LONELY FOR ME?

57

When I wasn't there
---When you weren't here

There's a "hearing"
in an auditorium we should
attend. About loneliness…

---about loneliness? Say no
    more! I confess my loneliness…

me too I do confess a case of this
lonelihood…

---you wear it everywhere.
Yes, I wear it in duress and out….

Remember when you thought "bicycle" before I
said "bicycle." That's how

---close our touchless touch,
our much-touched touching of
---mind?

No…
Spirit. Your Spirit came
paddling through dusk, one
tear crawling down its face,
an orange tea-flower growing behind it
on the riverbank. How lovely
that any flower grows…

PAUSE

---I keep waiting for something
    to tilt off axis to annihilate the both of us . . .

However heavy, the hour
has never been
wasted between us there, has not been

---a single minute for naught.
    We are sheer miracles!

Almost fish!

---Gliding through water we are nearly
    elk lowering our heads in the shadows
    of the Great Oak of the Silver Maple of the
    whole hoodlum forest. Would you like to

eat? Yes, I am quite hungry—

They Want to Know

(Two Voices)

They want to know what our daughter is doing
---She's pouring water from a stainless steel bowl into the marigolds

What are the bruises on her arms
---What are the bruises on her legs

Is that where the anger has gone

---Now she's rocking slowly in the chair, now looking through
the northern mesh

And now the eastern—there's the emerald ash

---What part of her has she abandoned?
The lonely
---or the hungry?

She eats again
---and drinks. She has a discernible body.

She's walking inside into the kitchen, pushing up the window
---She's walking back out, she's picking dandelions

Where is her body?
---Do you mean her mind?
I mean the mind of her body

---Her feet lightly graze the ground—she sits in the chair again,
    losing hair, bees whirring
    around her head…

Everything else of her strains away—

---Never meant to have a husband
That's her thought you caught!

---Hadn't she been married before?
To the Envelope of Emptiness?

---Not so devastating as that, no—
    she married a Gingko Leaf,

shadows of grackles skimming her face…
---The ancestral pull can be fatal

By the second shadow she'll have passed the flag—

Two Voices Contemplating Their Existence

Is she, are we, making a story
---of the speaker and Michiko. Of war?

And Richard and Michael and the four...?
---We are not making anything, we are

the story?
---We are a story, the lyric story....

Here's a strand spiraling out from the stars
---sober, neglected.

Another strand of music in her hair
---uncombed but washed.

Inconclusive, full of error, we are....
---(*Hear Hear!*)

full of love for being....
---(*Amen Amen!*)

In chorus: WE ARE

opaque, motionless
in her mind upon waking

---in her breath as she drifts to sleep
    as snow drifts into its shadow

in her scrambled stories....
---What story's not?

The authors have a way of "organizing."
---The letters do that themselves! Too much

meddling and insufficient
---heart!

We're critics floating in the sky!
---Real gentlepeople!!

Watch us hover over
---*Watch us never*

subside....

The Speaker Tells a Story. The Voices Ask a Question.

Was barreling down the road in a '77 silver Hornet station wagon. Almost comical. Could fit a passel of children and animals.

Under what sky? Was it glitterpicked? How many windows?

Many windows / daylight cut through/ my throat tightened / no blood / several snowbirds flew overhead—.

Where were you going?

You mean toward which personal loss was I heading?

PAUSE

I turned and turned the key turned the key/ sputtered and shook and stopped / turned the key again / the sky a cloudless ache / have you ever seen a blue ache / crossed through by snowbirds / no blood....

When the car finally started where were you going?

Barreling down the road in a '77 Hornet. Almost comical, heading toward the hospital, flying through stop signs, flying through squirrels, angular weeds shuddering I banged past....

And?

*9 miles to go, white Buick ahead, the driver driving the limits down the road I
was barreling, barreling 'til he slowed, slowed below the limits...*

???

*I honked I flashed my lights I yelled out the window I honked flashed yelled
"Move on.... Move on...." The birds fled the driver slowed, near to a halt....*

He didn't move to the shoulder?

*He gave me the finger before turning left. He was not thinking about private
loss—the sky ached, bright weeds angled up, sideways, frozen silver, the '77
Hornet barreling, weaving and honking in his rearview mirror on a road that
was otherwise*

quite empty.

Almost drained the road was. The birds didn't return.

When *do* we think about private loss, the private loss of other
drivers on the road?
When do we think about our own?

I wasn't thinking the driver wasn't budging he wasn't thinking—

did you ever make it to the hospital?

*He wasn't lying down on the bed, he was sitting up, his eyes closed, face
beautifully painless, his skin opaque.*

SILENCE

I got to the hospital late. I paused for a fatal minute at the gleaming doors...

[THE LAMP IS LIKE A CAPSIZED SHIP]
(Two Voices Muse Over the Speaker)

The lamp is like a capsized ship
---or like a lantern gone drunk

And she's to sleep by it
---or stare wide-eyed at its light askew

And she's to read to it
---to put it to sleep

And she's to dream in it
----warmly aglow as a leopard

whose body is shadow and light
---Whose body isn't?

She's missing again
---Where did she go?

Curled-in
---Is she spiraling?

Less energy than that…
---Will the bedsheets accommodate her?

She's alone in them, alone where she can
easily breathe

---despite the horrors the stretchers the gasping...?

How can anyone
---breathe easily.... She must

be still as a Bradford Pear in uneasy shadow...
---That tree that self-destructs that tree that neuters the real pear trees

What a blow it was so beautiful and erect at first—
---and she so lonely

Lonely as a cup
---Here is a card:

She needs the Lion today, the one who leaves
gold footprints in the marsh

[PINK FEATHER YOU WERE]
(The Voice Leads the Speaker into Deeper Reflection)

Pink feather you were
more yellow than pink,
the littler bones evident—
a massacred fish.
Shall I speak more
smoothly…. In what kind of light do you live?

Bruised.
---Can we begin at the hook?

A dream of fields, rivers
that led to the Caspian Sea
where horses swam
not terrified.
They spoke with large wild eyes.

When did I lose my belief…?

---In this?
In this. In them. The Forest.

---You hurried away from the forest, your voice feathering as you ran—
I was flying I kept telling myself I was flying

---you were hurrying, feathering away…

I was hurrying through the city my littler bones rattling
scraping past storefronts leaning into cement walls

---that could support you, that would not take up your space…
hard still things I could lean into just in case

---you fainted?
In case I fainted I was leaning as I hurried bones softly rattling and I hurried
out of

---fear of fainting?
Out of terror for my life something was chasing me…

---or shooing you away?
Yes, that's closer. Something shooing me away:

---Why did you lose your belief?

In forest?
---In forest and voice, in your voice of forest.

I was ashamed of my paucity, my creeping quiet, ashamed
---of your inability?

to stand and walk. Already I was curled
like a pill bug, I was
like a red-faced pill bug, always curled, blushing
at the slightest tap of kind attention,
repulsive as I was…

---repulsive as you felt….
Yes, repulsive as I felt.

---Repulsive as a reptile?
No, they are beautiful. Repulsive as a thing that couldn't ask.

---So you hurried and feathered....
I couldn't ask for milk...it was transformative my hurried feathering.

---Was it their looking that made you ugly?
It was their not looking.

---Did their words make you ugly?
Yes, the whole world was ugly to them and I was
---"part of it." You wrote that in a song once.

A song is another
heartbeat in the world.

---Is this enough for today?

The littler bones now inseparable from the larger—
they work beautifully together, slow and
in silence—.

THRILLING THE MOON'S COMPLETED FACE
(A Song from the Speaker)

Thrilling once the moon's completed face
      Rain rushed in, rushed back

Then the moon turned inward

*

I saw the moon in her singing dress
I saw the moon
           in her swinging dress
Swinging like a lantern
         before a bruise
Singing like a lantern
          as it silenced itself
I saw the moon in a wedding dress
I went out of my mind
        and into a cave

*

I saw the hidden cruelties
     of gems

even when not crushed underfoot
     or scattered by wind

I looked a gem in the eye

It didn't have hands
        but it trembled a lot

*

What was that about tenderness?
            That about hooves?

Where are Chagall's blue horses?
His soft naked people in rose-hip swoon, blurred moon…

Is it the moon or human at stake?

13 years "married"—which cave were we in…was it
you alone? Was it I? Who

traveled where?

THE STORY OF THE SPEAKER & THE STINKBUG
(Two Voices)

Travel beyond this white fountain to the tiny stream of childhood
...where she pillaged stones from the water to clear passage?

Must there be harm to clear passage?
...Seems inevitable.

And now the shameful moss thickens—"white on hanging wire."
...Did the thousand voices emanate from the stinkbug she smashed?

Everything tasted stinkbug—coffee, oatmeal, water...
...the tiny stream from childhood?

She doused her hands in it, but never drank, it was a trickle.
...What were the voices saying when you weren't human?

Sorry sorry sorry sorry sorry sorry sorry sorry
...Can we take those sorries to the woods, to the tiny stream, can we

excise them? Expunge? Every mouthful she takes she tastes stinkbug.
...Its spirit flew into her mouth as she slept. Four gunshots woke her,
a signal.
Were the four gunshots that woke her a signal?

We'd rather the bells from stone churches—
...rather the trains in snow—
     In chorus: WE KNOW NOTHING

Why do they yank children from their tiny streams?
...So they won't scream.... Did she become the thing she smashed?

The stinkbug?
...Too neat an equation.

The white fountain thinks so hard its water crenulates
...and I wish hard for Snow—Eternal Zhivago Snow.

Hasn't this before been your wish? Or is it mine?
...Ours, dearheart, as every exchange, as who-says-what is essentially moot.

Is the stinkbug taste fading?
...It's more of her life rushing in—

A Bout of Terrible Shrieking

(The Speaker Confides in a Voice)

I must escort my children through the gate

…It might turn red with your passage

Or silver?

…A thin hope

Under a small earl-star, I walked down the hill

…toward the Gardens?

Yes—two owls flew so low their wings nicked the telephone pole—

…Then?

I saw the silver shadows as they passed

They leave some shining in the branches, some they take in flight

But they themselves are not shadows?

…No, your owls are no longer shadows—

Carrying their exact selves…are they symbols?

…Not symbols, not representatives—Witnesses

*Two witnesses of my heart flying swiftly through trees
into the Gardens of Shadows*

…The same Gardens where you wed another's Shadow

And not my own

…And not your own

Let us pass through the red gate—I'll carry one guardian—the clay sun

…And I'll carry another—dark plastic Ninja and his bandaged wrist

The Speaker Shares Her Fierce Wish with the Voices

…Are you near, Comrades?

Indeed! Why so enlarged today—a veritable Super Bloodflower Moon you are!

…I am wishing fierce—willing the young cat to be alive, harnessing the Great Four Winds to help her stay, inhaling the breath of creeping jenny, hellebore, woodruff, the tougher plants, I am packing my bones with stones to keep steady, bathing in diamonds, planting forests….

All that force to keep a small being alive?

…What being is small? Every being harnessed to another and another and soon…

all the horses die?

…Or worse. The world goes down. My second secret father is traveling farther away….

Have you been a good daughter?

…I have been a peculiar daughter.

Injured? Mistaken? Insufficient?

PAUSE

Did you see the HUMAN BODY book?

…Lowest book in the pile on the sun-cracked shelf.

ONE MILLION THINGS it said on the spine, illustrations galore—
tendons, bones, tiny nerves.

*…My second secret father is becoming a husk, his breath both smaller and
larger as he ebbs—.*

A matchstick lay next to the HUMAN BODY book

…fallen from the pocket of a child who wanted to die.

Did he want to burn the book?

*…The book was irrelevant, he felt, but my secret father wrote enough books
to make a threefold tower, enough books to be the walls and bridges and birds
of a city—.*

We knew something of his work—his affinity for maples and squirrels,
roadkill and dancing.

Michiko would have loved him.

…This is not a prayer, nor is it a meditation.

Where is your secret father now?

*…On the East River, leisurely rowing a boat, the sun in his hair, his hair
newly-returned….*

And the fish?

*…A slew of fish flying after him—the slower he rows, the harder it is for
them to catch him….*

Imagine that! Fish trying to catch a human!

...He endowed upon them his spirit as he did every bird—

as he does the lake of his vanishing—

THE REAL WISH AVE

Is there a real Wish Ave?
---*Sure. Between Payne Rd and 86ᵗʰ, west of Ditch*

PAUSE

---*My real husband is reading Lucretius*
By real you mean true?

---*By real, I mean real to himself,*
    to the void, to
    the smegma that pushes
    against void

Are you sick of imposters?—
---*Imposters posturing themselves, posting anything everything*
    what they're eating, how they're loving, hating....
    There is no forest to it even when they post a
forest—

A book is $1/16$ a forest depending on the width
---*flinging names and lines around me swirling titles round their heads*
    like American lassos

Where is the quiet comradery between human and book?
Even our goodness is made into parody....

Sink back here with me with your real husband. Let's read
a line together unposted, unpostable:
"And that these same ne'er cease in interchange…" Lucretius sayeth

---HEAVY DUTY quoth the cardboard box at my feet

"Unto the stars of ethereal world
Which in no wise at all the germs can do."

[SHE HAS MOVED UPSTAIRS]

(Two Voices)

Has she moved upstairs!?

---Shhhh. I don't want to disturb her lest she...

stop in her tracks?

---Too far gone for that but watch her watching

the exquisite crescent moon—!

---And the planet directly above it—is it Jupiter?

Never. Venus forever, Venus above the crescent...

---I love speaking to you.

PAUSE

When we watch her, I'm shy as a horse in the moonlight....

---Now she is entering the dark space moving motionless....

Once she moved frantically though paralyzed

---when she lived underground, when she didn't

live in a house with floors for chrissakes!!

---And tonight with great solemnity through the soft haze of white sage

she carries a thoughtful pile of blankets,

---three extra pillows, a modest-sized clock.

She is padding around upstairs,

---placing a small notebook under a white lamp.

People do that all the time you know...

---people, yes. This for her has the sanctity of first.

A trillion dull and dazzling cities she's slept in to figure

---how to raise herself, how to eat, and now

how to traverse upstairs how to move fluidly

---from one level to the next.

Is that what you mean by integration?

---Beautiful Emblem of Thought you are.

Are we the working parts of her Mind

or two glass-flowers in a blue shaft of light...

BREAK

PRELUDE

...did he whisper it or did he say it
without intention but with
meaning: the child hunched in the cupboard,
crammed with canned beans and soups, behind one
tin of jackfruit: "I feel
safe in small spaces." This was the beginning

of the pandemic, was that when he said it or was he
lodged in there earlier because even before
a pandemic there was a Great Need
for safety, for a cupboard—. Was he eight or
ten? Did it really happen? His bruised child-
knees sometimes kneeling in there, a small hand
holding a flashlight. It must have been
warm, the stove right next to the cupboard
door, jars and cans and boxes of food stacked high....
He even took books in there with him
and a water bottle....

Surviving like that was that the beginning
of the pandemic or was he lodged in there earlier
out of the Great Need for safety for structures—?

Where were the parents?

PAUSE

--*"Everything is Loss" the child said*
Tiredly, very tiredly
his adult eyes
Darkly shining from that small cupboard
space, his
Space—when we looked
in, when we saw him there
some world collapsed--

GREBE

"We are gathered here today" the dear hostas breathe beloved,
eight huddled around a stump, tightfurled where juniper berries
in winter gather their smoky voices. My beloveds heregathered dearly
in this small square yard, beloved are the heaps and dribbles of stone
and dirt. Dearly beloved are we all gathered here by cardinal
and northern window and blunt lily-to-be. "Dear gatherers"
the hostas whisper, strapped in like small green parasols...
their hushed breath the clearest breath today—

A blue light travels briefly over the meadow

      What is my condition now that I've outlived my context?
What is my new law of being? What is
      the framework?

I inhabit the blurry middle.

Will this new law of being be restrictive
      or permissive? How will we
breathe? Blue light pauses in the tangled song
      of wet crickets where amid night-violets, those loving
curlers, I stand—.

They'd cut off the man's feet, they'd
laid him down.

***

     Years after that horror   yellow roses thrashing
in opposition near the painting of the blighted blue mask   its red
streak of mouth in the dark
constricting world of the frame   then
one pale figure rising—
     in hospital gowns in cities and villages
many figures rising—

Are you all right are you all right alright alright in there?

***

In my dream there were three tasks:
      I folded a magic basketball in half
      I stitched a dress out of an accordion while it was breathing
heavy by the sea, heavy by the sea…
      I was jolted out of the third harsh vigilance. My fivefold insect's
eye:
Is the child breathing

The cards of March were deathly: a punctured eyeball pinioned
by yarn
And a blue tree floating in air without roots
The water in the backyard rose and did not sink
All colors took on their neighbors'

      I remember the respirator, I remember how it made the man's
hospital gown balloon out, subside, balloon. Nobody was stopping it
though he was dead. We were transfixed by
breath moving without a breather

The child drew the Magician card

***

Her name was Windflower but we called her Flower
      My favorite dog of the meadow
White as a star in snow turning her head around to make sure
I was there

At 3 a.m. I think of her, stark in my own life, as you at 3 a.m. are stark
in yours

Maybe we're all stars then. Disjointed, sharp, too bleakly bright to see
ourselves anywhere but in vast outer spaces emptying, timeless as she
in all softness,
the memory-blur at 3 a.m.

      Her concerned eyes caught my throat.
      All dogs are inward, all hounds of the hamlet gone
      inward now—.

The way the petal fell, the way white meant contagion now, white with
    red flecks
the gasp in the brush, the way blossoms looked
like crowns, crowns like
a virus.

      The only way to talk about childhood was to talk about woods
and meadow
      and fox and deer and the sycamore at a vast distance. The ash
tree scripted over
      by emerald borers. *D*-shaped wounds. The many contagions....

And the lake that much farther away—.

"What will you name her?" they asked

Windflower but we'll call her Flower, it's easier to call her that way

****

The respirator takes on a life of its own
The respirator takes a life of its own
The respirator takes a life

Petals fall, fill in the cracks
   Petals will, wall in the cracks
Petals, small investigators of breath

doubling over—
   in a gust—

Beforelife the title of the book that could've been Celan or Valentine
        appeared before me before I knew my new context

weeks later behind the tiny square window of the kitchen
        three black-capped chickadees appear
        thieves of the heart

what is there to ask of them   They live in a village
        of breath   Remember the breathing
that had no breather

I wanted to add a faded red house
        to the view
weeks after watching the film where the peach-soft
        girl gets blown up in a car

in the middle of her joy mid the free passage of her joyful love
        weeks after watching the film my tears begin

unstoppably as they might have in real life
        where the mouth and jaw ache

she was within a dream
        the soft-faced girl in the Italian film walking with children

a young teacher a child herself tendril of life the only tenderness
        there   I dry-eyed   watched the film again decades later

during the pandemic   shrewd   without despair

but over the weeks she appeared and re-appeared at 3 a.m.

lifting off her soft shirt in the blowing wind   billowing up
tears without prohibition

I am going inward you said I am inward more inward I am moving away

***

Gone the man with stumps for legs   Gone the breathing
machine

I will enter this rain into the registry of tears

Remember the respirator how it made his gown balloon it was the first part of
day

Grebe is the bird of today
Her oily feathers spanned flat   the pattern of tire tread
where no cars had sped
Her fractured eye fixed on us as she sinks

        The whisperers were not in love they were dying they were
whispering
            as a way to breathe

For them, for you going inward again, I grieve
for the child pounding walls again: grieve, grieve
            with me, Grebe—

Small oval crystals on my doorstep
   qualify as the light of this day. I first piled them
in a transparent heap the shape of an anthill
   soon jostled out of place,
many fell into the grass magnifying the blades
   unintentionally, atonally,
as unintentionality has been so long my song
   having had no mind to move with the swift deadly force
of consciousness. Every force, every movement deadly:
   watch the lively steps of the green fly, its arabesques, its
disco wings and the distraction of honeysuckle blooms hung
from bloodless canopies,
   the killings going unnoticed undercover.
In the high bright air: "Rules," you said…

"We have to have rules" and you stepped away I
stepped away and from that safe distance we could see how
large we'd become, almost enormous with hunger that
had its own plan. We listened for other voices—.
      Red star above us, shrubs noiselessly coupling,
the simple plan of the sun, shadows enlarging, swelling
around the edges—. We'd been reading from
 a large pink book about a crystal city shatterproof
though the crystal is as glass, delicate, in peril,
but immortal. It holds and reflects so perfectly
the world becomes black, a black shine we live inside
together in that book, that crystal book. "Rules" you said.
"What we can and cannot do." I touch the crystals
on my doorstep, leave the others in the grass.
When I pass through the door they without moving pass too—

What was the rule for the man with stumps for legs, the man

       whose feet they had cut off? What is the rule for
our breathing, machines

billowing the gowns around us? For those transfixed by that,
who need

to be pulled away—.

The rules become less about contact, more about listening
The real rule is to pay attention to the dignity of light
When breath gathers badly, stop moving
Let breath become a meadow, pulsing with froglets,
ferret out the hurt, heed the sorcery of the lake
The rule of yellow roses, their withdrawn throats, secret
layers of their minds
The rules no longer about nakedness—but about being too
heavily clothed,
too masked. The rules have to do with bare hands in dirt
Rules determined by gardens, gardens by a river, by a church,
Rules of garden and river and church all the same, all correct
At the pearl edge of the downcast sea correct, all
correct—

BREAK

[Why aren't you speaking to me?]

(Two Voices)

Why aren't you speaking to me?
---The eldercat caught a young rabbit....

When?
---Last night inside the electric light
of the Sturgeon Moon—full and veiny blue but distant.

Are you afraid of Memory—?
---How so?

How it sinks, anchoring nothingness, every pore widemouthed
before it....
---Does it want to undo us?

It wants to reveal us—.
---Harm harm harm ALARM

We can walk gently there
---only if there's a forest—

a forest and a darkling stream, yes!
---Why are tears straggling down your face?

Do I want to be the darkling stream?
---No...

all the stones their little faces downward turned.
---You're speaking in Morse—

I'm speaking remorsefully....
---You're somehow human after all....

Nothing is sacred about us—only what is between us
---and what we convey. How we link air-to-air

with "the finest of ease"—how we fly, linking wings with
the wet hills of sea—.
---Now I am speaking to you—

every voice a bee
---starved for a throat-scorching sweetness—.

And now I can hear your velvet burr

I Love My Brother

(The Speaker Sings)

I.

The tree is a feather. I believe everything you declare.
The cat kissed a star he'd caught in his paw.
Loneliness in a leg at rest or hurrying through a tunnel
while hitched to a hip it didn't choose. The blinders on the horses
in Central Park are maddening. And the turrets spin wildly while
we sleep. I can do nothing about this world but weep
or celebrate. Though yesterday I became a piece of bark
that had been dislodged from a tree and laid to rest. The people
cleverly used me as a walkway. I am immune to cleverness.
Am I a village flooded by orange poppies? Has Milkweed undone
my mind. There is no answer in the hall. Every fern turns into
a question. There's not a mirror not forsaken. We rush to save the sliver.
Neglect is a crumb the pigeons skitter for.
There's a skittish heart in a state of undress. Latch onto me, moss.
The tenderness of your root-nubs, the velvet perspective. We carry our arrows
between our teeth. We rest as blackly as we can to connect with the universe.

II.

I am not trying anymore to try.
Tried things are sad and tired.
The quiet fervor of bulbs pushing up
is one sacred square in my heart.

Spring pulls me down wet, barbed
as a nettle, my rattling husk lost, lost
the favorite song of the wind.
Why pretend anymore I am not disconnected
or divisive as the rest? I make walls
out of petals....
Once I thought I was not pretending, once I dreamed
I was imagining. The soft g always helps me shudder
into Quiet, my original language.
I'm no trumpet. My noises scurry
away into billows of dust, frantic, hungry.
What am I doing
to save anything? I am not trying anymore to try.
The rabbit's long ears wilt over its skull. Someone compares
them to leaves. Someone else says "compare" is one way
to care. There's an insect in the interstice that has no fingers,
but it is signaling for a mate
or it is dying,
its body a delicate wire hooked to a few translucent petals
that are its wings. I don't need to touch it
to believe in love. I love my brother— he is often the bearer—
this time his hands fill with "the last fireflies!" he cries—.
Without fireflies
or birds, what is the sky?

THE VOICES CHATTER ABOUT THE SPEAKER'S AFOREMENTIONED SONG

What is the sky? she cried.
---No, that was her brother crying.

Are you crying?
---What are we doing

to save anything!? We're crying out—!
Heady as dead winter hydrangea,

the light clipping at the big ghostly bloom,
ghost-robins carrying dead grass over

---the living! We're crying out—
as the living grass!

"Harebrained" comes to mind when I think of us. Angelic
and harebrained.
Rabbits bounding through meadows' bright winter bones.

---She might be "disconnected, divisive as the rest."
Are we helping her cohere?

---She of the three hearts!
She of the brooding skull.

THE SPEAKER TELLS THE STORY OF HER MENTOR
for Gerald Stern

Last night the Silence at 3 a.m. wasn't Theater
and it wasn't a book....

...Has he stopped reading?

He has a new way of traveling...he leans into his walker...noiselessness
without stealth.

...(Was your young cat found injured?

Not found at all)... "I've gone into hiding" he said
somewhat fiercely, holding onto his walker.

...Now he seems softer

his face out of focus—nowhere-eyes. A white jowlish blur of iris—
his backyard smelled of early childhood.

...Now you sound like Theater.

His first abandonment was his sister...he made the ink go quiet
around her name.

...He'd gone into hiding...did he say more beyond that?

That might have been the last urgent thing he said to me....

...How did you answer?

"All your friends gone" I said. "Galway, Stanley..." my voice trailing off...

...then?

*He returned to a cheerful light, pointed to the portrait someone had done
of him, sang an old French ballad from before the war, gestured toward
a plate of cookies, then he took my hand,
and held it through half a story, half a joke....*

Did you ever move from that one room?

*We took an elevator down to the basement where his books and papers
were...the window barred, he could see only dust.*

...Did he speak more then?

No.

...Was it a terrible Silence?

There was no traffic, not a wren or mating owl—it was a clear space—

...for his Travels?

An open runway—

THE SPEAKER SAYS TO ONE VOICE: I KEPT THE BROKEN OBJECTS

I kept the broken objects but didn't fill the cracks with gold
ignorant of Golden joinery didn't know to seal them
seal with gold the cracked colors of an antique rose

…You are drowsed by Time again

I'm admiring the tender hearts of seconds
quickly ticking

…You were taking the Pulse of Hummingbirds?

Of sparrows—still horrified by the Creed to destroy them

…What if life isn't sacred

What if only the sky—

…the boneless bounteous sky

I miss Michiko, I miss her plantings, the new neighbors plant too but she

…wore gloves, she was a Doctor of Flora & Fauna

Where is she now

…Where are you?

That is my best friend's most famous, most useful question
I'm somewhere close enough that you can hear me whisper

...Can you hear her hushed whisper as she hurriedly walks her dog?

YES! Michiko's voice hasn't vanished...

...Has Tom's?
No!

...Has Lucy's?
No!

...Have your Grandparents'?
No! No!

...Some voices speak from the throat, others from the nose
My favorite person's voice speaks from the Hollows

...you mean the torso?
& the feet...as Lorca's poems do

...Let's go ride seven dark horses with Vallejo, with Jerry!
Let's sail off on Baudelaire's ragweed boat—!

...through the widening Emily-mind—
& Sappho's Hour of Gold.

Bright Red Spot

(Two Voices Consider Mortality)

To see the bright red spot beneath the dead rat's head
---bright even in December rain,

is to understand the red halo
of death that frames our face from the get-go, nothing to do
with goodness

---has to do with having a brother
      who notices: he says,

          "I mean there was a soft white chest. The rat was on its side."
          Troublous and beautiful both.

This makes me think of a far-off sister,
her translations, devotions

---as intimate as any....
      The brother's mother called that rat image "marring."

Did she mean jarring?
---She meant the sight of a soft white chest and blood

marred her day...
---while it is music that marries the breath to the body....

Jazz is "tiny enough for that ledge."

---The music?

All music and its tiny notes climbing, falling invisibly
but not dying.

The sister dropped the book in the Hudson River
in a December rain,

the pages loosening in the current
headed toward the mouth of the Cousin Sea.

[TO KNOW THAT MICHIKO RETURNED]

(Two Voices)

To know that Michiko returned
to her country
was a small inconclusive comfort.

---At least it wasn't Florida.

Realtors can be liars:
Dream house! Dream house for sale!
Dream person derailed.

---You blocked my voice with the end stop.

Unintentionally. The despair
lingers…long after you wade through the stones

---and trash
        of upheaval. Michiko moved
            from the neighborhood after we'd known her walking

for over a decade. A silver-veined whiteness
piled on her head like the snow
on Mount Shirouma

---recrystallized!

And the glass jar of larvae

116

Michiko carried in both hands

---to protect them. The clarity of their casing
        just before emerging. Returning home
        is one emergence. Leaving home
        is another. Michiko returned and left

simultaneously. Such was her
power. She proffered flowers and shrubs
to everyone in the neighborhood—daylilies, viburnum . . .
She planted two redbud trees

---on our land, for us, the silver-veined whiteness
        of her hair as she crouched, patting soil
        around the saplings, she sang

when she spoke, bending low
to the earth as a practice, she knew grief

---not neglect. A chrysalis might
        drop from its branch, it might be
        eaten by ants or rats, devoured by
        wasps. Remember when you were

a chrysalis?

---How you disguised yourself as a dead
        black hairstreak, then an orange-tipped bud,
        curled leaf from speckled wood.

On her first warm walk one Spring
Michiko took off her cap and we saw

the silver-veined whiteness of her hair

---as though she'd molted, the jolting
      fear, unspoken, that soon she'd
      depart, one way or the other....

We, too—

---no, please don't.

Now you're the one putting an end stop on things....

---Can't we converse this way forever?

Maybe *sotto voce* from beneath the grass?

---When you say grass I despair less—

Japanese Silver Grass, Japanese Blood Grass
---hath Michiko in her new land—

Big Bluestem and Bottlebrush Grass for us
---and the starlings' eternal murmurations—

It All Happened So Quickly
(The Speaker Sees Herself)

In the swirl of the day
>   *within an hour daylily-trumpets not yet raised*
>   *within an hour a striped bird rinsed off in the glassy creek*
an hour in which
I lay down hard and her soft hair came to light

>   *soft hair of the ill*
>   *"soft hair"of the graces, the grasses*
>   *(by graves could only be so soft)*

softness

>   *hovering above a face, above*
>   *her heavy eyes…*

>   *"Got the will to love?"—her face too gaunt—*

>   *not the will to live—*

Water in that Young song, Fire too—

>   *Loved. She was Loved.*
>   *Down hard on the floor I lay and her soft hair*
came to light
>   *and with it her eyes*
>   *her gaunt face*

merciless merciless…
to herself merciless—.

PAUSE

("Did she have a body?" the Voices asked.)

I planted 7 saplings today
        fiery purple lanterns
        of columbine

  fat birds on delicate branches,

        basil thick with spice too fierce
        to hold in the mouth

(The Voices murmured "It can be hard to hold any flavor.…")

When I lay hard on the ground, the instructor said:
"Stay, through the discomfort, stay here."

("Did she say *stay* with kindness? Will *stay*
be your lullaby?" the Voices asked.)

        Her soft hair came to light
        framing her gaunt face.…

        Her mouth I didn't notice—was it a slit or all gone or just

a small hole.

(The Voices asked "How did it happen so fast
that she returned?")

> Loved. She was Loved.
> And my soft hair
>
> came to light—

The Speaker Makes a Pronouncement

I've come upon a Wish

---Avenue?

No, I've discovered my body. It's floating over cities and fields and cows,
floating over other bodies, floating
over Wish Ave and a house there with a room and a table upon which rests
a square cake.

---Are you weary to be thus suspended? Is your wish to come down?

The Light here illuminates the tiny cold cathedrals within each bone, look
close: a veritable cathedral inside some of them....

---Is that why you wear a coat and a hat?

My hair's been falling softly asunder my hair's the snow the pollen the
ruminations of dust my hair's breathily falling softly asunder...

---We didn't realize the hair drifting around us was yours we didn't
realize how widely you've been traveling....

All of us leaving our parcels of skin, leaving our naked cells everywhere not
out of neglect not out of caring

---but haplessly so...

heapingly haplessly so

----Should we pause here to allot us a moment
of wistfulness?

---And wishfulness that we may endure
hairless or not?

---Whether our coats, our hats blow away—.
The heart has no eyes it's all feelers it communes through vibrations,
rhythms....

---Can we return to the house on Wish Ave, can we return to the room
with the cake?
Yes, please. I've missed it....

PAUSE

PAUSE
PAUSE

I've come upon an Understanding:

Inside my body there is an empty square—as though the cake
had been cut right out of it!

But I am here as both container and
containment. The empty square

is private knowledge.

---Shall we rest now?

Let's rest floatingly my wisps of hair falling around us . . .
---they make a beautiful bed to dream upon

WITNESSING IT
(One Voice Asks the Speaker Another Question)

Why are you sitting outside in the snow without a coat?
---*I want to witness it*

If you don't—?
---*I have to watch it at the critical moment or how will I know*
that it happened

When the last splint cracks
and the thing is disemboweled,
it lies heavy on the ground

---*No p.s., no whisper…*
while the green flies rummage and bustle

---*while the woodpeckers, the doves…*

get to the hollow places, they are
---*getting to the hollow spaces but not for naught*

There's as much life in dead wood as there is in the living
---*And the hollow where that gnarled arm was?*

Becomes a clearing—

Remember when you stayed awake all night to watch the Luna Moth
take off in first flight?

---Those hours, those speckled hours, it twitched and strained
        its wings like leaflets in low wind,
        staggering and spinning over the ground
        below the young maple

PAUSE

---I didn't sleep
No, but in that minute you looked away—
---that immeasurable minute

it finally flew
        past the young maple's dead leaves

---where grubs live!
And the wild snail rests…

THE CHILDREN RETURN, THE SPEAKER REPORTS

Here I am, Voices, I am no longer floating—
      I made my nest
                unslept in it

The children in danger
      were running by moonlight
I am no longer floating
      the vineyards were burning
I must use my arms, find my hands—
      four dogs in flames baying and crying...

Let them have their struggle / smoky white skull
floating at dusk under the bridge
in a forest / drop down / stop / let
them fear / two pebbles
by an ice pond / let them walk again—

I walk again / they will ask
what tree is this? / I will say
Green Ash / the cupboard will fill
with cans of stew, bone broth—
and the children will sleep in their beds

just one small blue light on—
children again
      with a mother

Something was coming—someone
gone

We remain alive
through the dreaming eye—

The Voices Come out of the Woodwork for Solace

"We're the underswell, soft
as whale-shadow but with more movement—

we're swelling and welling
beneath her,

we're lifting her up—
(Don't you feel larger, daughter?

Can you feel your stomach?)—
we live inside the floating night,

our experience is dreams when not
nightmares. We break

and cohere. Ours is a perfect
union because we can

have conversation. We fracture,
we kiss, we lap around each other,

we can drift a little while
in vast uninterruptible quiet, green

and lavender, but we always turn and re-
turn. No blacking out in corners, no

hurtling into ditches. We are
the counterparts—

we reflect, we sing
her encounters. We murmur

about her like concerned
parents in the low-lit fields

of living rooms. We murmur
in watery candlelight, the light

murmurs too. Aren't we after all her true
parentage? Isn't this why she's sought

us though we've been here
the whole time—

this might not comfort her
this might just carry her—.

Buoy, hoist, and
underswell, we are the more internal

soft-rocking waves, here when she begins
to tip over—. We marry stormy water,

marry the wind, the atmosphere, the icy
current, we marry her to the

world. Welcome."

[I CAN'T BELIEVE YOU TOLD THEM!]

(Two Voices)

I can't believe you told them!
---About the Hawk fluttering, striped wings in the creek for a wash,
soft chest?

No—that we are always here, always ready to speak…
---(I'd never seen such tenderness in a Hawk)

and that we are waiting in the shadow of the Buckeye,
the Redbud, a Swamp Oak sapling….

--- I thought of the Red Tulip, black dots in its wide mouth—

a flower! A flower to represent us!
---Its boldness, assertiveness—.

Or an Indigo Bunting or a Tulip Tree's rooty scouting—.

---Can't just turn on an image like a spigot, pal!
We're all thirsty here.

---I might go into hiding in the desert….
First follow me to the riverbank.

---What is it you're sporting?
Sycamore limb and Ragweed….

---Is that river-shale in your hair?!
Close—Blue Asters and Marsh Marigolds....

---to keep you warm!
Here's a stone for your mouth, one for mine.

---What about the Red Tulip?
It'll hold our world in place.

---And our endless conversations?
They'll let it loose—

LONG PAUSE

VOICES: *Child, let's get out of here*

SPEAKER: *but there's a sunshower in a dandelion field*

We can bring that with us...
---*and the stone birdbath?*
Yes.
---*Then what are we leaving behind?*
Trauma.
---*Say again?*
We're leaving behind splinters, a chasm where a staircase
should be, the "total breakdown of the woods."
---*How are we to move?*
Follow our voices. Dark has its velvet too—
---*Do you love me?*
Yes.

---Will you warm my hands?
Yes, yes.
---My coat is unbuttoned, the wind is cold and sharp....
We will button your coat and hold your hands.
---If I'm too quiet what will you do?
We will listen.
---Do I need to ask permission to leave this place?
We are walking with you. We are here—.
---Are there houses whose inhabitants are not only shadows?
Yes, those are the houses that carry and hold light,
that will carry and hold you....
---Then what are we leaving behind?
An arctic palace, a sealed-in suffering, the dark that is not
velvet

BRIDGE

[Four strawberries I drop into your drinking glass]

(The Poet)

Four strawberries I drop into your drinking glass
     in honor of the moon they call "strawberry,"

wild, small, dim-lit, kept behind the floating mist,
a pinkish door in the darkened sky—

     "the only grace" it seems
"in the disordered city" of our feverish world.

     Before the Evaporation, under my writing desk I stored
a slim bottle, pale-green Portuguese wine. We lived

     in a small yellow house by the sea
of rushing hydrangea and allium, tides of creeping jenny
glowing beneath— .

     All we had was love and fear—nowhere
to release them—. The night overstocked, thick sweet shock of lilacs.

     In the stricken air, the bottle of Portuguese wine
poised—openmouthed, cork-less, its glassed-in green-gold sea
in abeyance.

     You take out the next book,
and then—in fear and love—we read.

ACKNOWLEDGMENTS

(Some of the poems were published with different titles or as different versions)

Bennington Review: "The Speaker Shares a Story with One Voice"
The Ex-Puritan: "The Speaker Tells a Story. The Voices Ask a Question"
The Glacier: "Witnessing It: One Voice Asks the Speaker Another Question," "Two Voices Dispute Harmony Harmoniously," "The Story of the Speaker & the Stinkbug"
Guesthouse: "Grebe"
The Kenyon Review: "I Love My Brother," "Ire," "The Speaker Runs through Shadows"
Laurel Review: "Some Other Musings by the Voices"
Poem-a-Day: "[The lamp is like a capsized ship]"
Porlock New Poetry: "[Why aren't you speaking to me?]"

Love to Jacqueline Oliva, La Prima Editrice Mia, La Mia Bellissima Mamma.

And to my dear trio of wise, resilient readers: for each: a Royal Hoopoe Bird and: Lamb's-ear & Hydrangea for David Stanford, Blue Orchids & Deep Purple Lilacs for Dana Roeser, and for Earl, Bleeding Hearts & Scorpion Grasses.

Recent Titles from Alice James Books

Autobiomythography of, Ayokunle Falomo
Old Stranger: Poems, Joan Larkin
I Don't Want To Be Understood, Joshua Jennifer Espinoza
Canandaigua, Donald Revell
In the Days That Followed, Kevin Goodan
Light Me Down: The New & Collected Poems of Jean Valentine, Jean Valentine
Song of My Softening, Omotara James
Theophanies, Sarah Ghazal Ali
Orders of Service, Willie Lee Kinard III
The Dead Peasant's Handbook, Brian Turner
The Goodbye World Poem, Brian Turner
The Wild Delight of Wild Things, Brian Turner
I Am the Most Dangerous Thing, Candace Williams
Burning Like Her Own Planet, Vandana Khanna
Standing in the Forest of Being Alive, Katie Farris
Feast, Ina Cariño
Decade of the Brain: Poems, Janine Joseph
American Treasure, Jill McDonough
We Borrowed Gentleness, J. Estanislao Lopez
Brother Sleep, Aldo Amparán
Sugar Work, Katie Marya
Museum of Objects Burned by the Souls in Purgatory, Jeffrey Thomson
Constellation Route, Matthew Olzmann
How to Not Be Afraid of Everything, Jane Wong
Brocken Spectre, Jacques J. Rancourt
No Ruined Stone, Shara McCallum
The Vault, Andrés Cerpa
White Campion, Donald Revell
Last Days, Tamiko Beyer
If This Is the Age We End Discovery, Rosebud Ben-Oni
Pretty Tripwire, Alessandra Lynch
Inheritance, Taylor Johnson

Alice James Books is committed to publishing books that matter. The press was founded in 1973 in Boston, Massachusetts to give women access to publishing. As a cooperative, authors performed the day-to-day undertakings of the press. The press continues to expand and grow from its formative roots, guided by its founding values of access, excellence, inclusivity, and collaboration in publishing. Its mission is to publish books that matter and preserve a place of belonging for poets who inspire us. AJB seeks to broaden our collective interpretation of what constitutes the American poetic voice and is dedicated to helping its artists achieve purposeful engagement with broad audiences and communities nationwide. The press was named for Alice James, sister to William and Henry, whose extraordinary gift for writing went unrecognized during her lifetime.

Designed by Pamela A Consolazio
PRINCIPAL CREATIVE DIRECTOR

Spark
design

Printed by Versa Press